Let's Jump Rope

By Sarah Hughes

Welcome
Books

Children's Press
A Division of Grolier Publishing
New York / London / Hong Kong / Sydney
Danbury, Connecticut

Photo Credits: Cover and all photos by Thaddeus Harden
Contributing Editors: Mark Beyer and Eliza Berkowitz
Book Design: Michael DeLisio

Visit Children's Press on the Internet at:
http://publishing.grolier.com

Library of Congress Cataloging-in-Publication Data

Hughes, Sarah, 1964-
    Let's jump rope / by Sarah Hughes.
      p. cm. — (Play time)
    Includes bibliographical references and index.
    Summary: Simple text and illustrations show children enjoying playing jump rope.
    ISBN 0-516-23114-6 (lib. bdg.) — ISBN 0-516-23039-5 (pbk.)
    1. Rope skipping—Juvenile literature. [1. Rope skipping.] I. Title.

  GV498.H84 2000
  796.2—dc21

                                                          00-025909

Contents

My name is Christina.

I like to jump rope.

5

Sometimes I jump rope **alone**.

I start with the rope behind me.

7

I **swing** it over my head.

I jump when it comes down to my feet.

9

I jump with both feet.

I like to see how many jumps
I can do without stopping.

11

Sometimes I jump rope with my friends, Michelle and Sarah.

Michelle and I hold the **ends** of the rope.

We swing the rope and Sarah jumps in the **middle**.

We like to sing songs while we jump rope.

Jumping rope is lots of fun!

15

Look!

The rope has hit Sarah's feet.

She could not jump over the **spinning** rope.

Now it is Michelle's turn.

I spin the rope with Sarah.

Michelle likes to jump on one foot.

Sometimes two of us jump rope.

I tie one end to a **rail**.

This is our favorite way to jump rope.

21

New Words

alone (uh-**lown**) by yourself

ends (**endz**) the last parts of something

middle (**mid**-dul) in the center

rail (**rayl**) a bar used to hold things up

spinning (**spin**-ing) turning around and around

swing (**swing**) to move back and forth

To Find Out More

Books

Jewels: Children's Play Rhymes
by Shelley Harwayne
Mondo Publishing

Jump Rope Magic
by Afi Scruggs
Scholastic, Incorporated

Jump Rope Rhymes
by Ellen Keller
Golden Books Family Entertainment

Web Sites

Jump Into A Healthy Life
http://tqjunior.advanced.org/5407
This site teaches kids that jumping rope is good for the heart, as well as fun. Learn new skills, take a quiz, and check out the links section.

United States Amateur Jump Rope Federation
www.usajrf.org
The official site of the USAJRF. Learn about jump rope events. See pictures of jumpers in action, and learn a new skill.

Index

About the Author

Sarah Hughes is from New York City and taught school for twelve years. She is now writing and editing children's books. In her free time, she enjoys running and riding her bike.

Reading Consultants

Kris Flynn, Coordinator, Small School District Literacy, The San Diego County Office of Education

Shelly Forys, Certified Reading Recovery Specialist, W.J. Zahnow Elementary School, Waterloo, IL

Peggy McNamara, Professor, Bank Street College of Education, Reading and Literacy Program